BENDING TOWARD HEAVEN

Allotment with Sunflower

Vincent van Gogh, Paris, 1887
Van Gogh Museum, Amsterdam
(Vincent van Gogh Foundation)

Bending Toward Heaven

Poems After the Art of Vincent van Gogh

Sharon Fish Mooney

RESOURCE *Publications* • Eugene, Oregon

BENDING TOWARD HEAVEN
Poems After the Art of Vincent van Gogh

Copyright © 2016 Sharon Fish Mooney. All rights reserved. Except for brief quotations in critical publications or reviews, no part of this book may be reproduced in any manner without prior written permission from the publisher. Write: Permissions, Wipf and Stock Publishers, 199 W. 8th Ave., Suite 3, Eugene, OR 97401.

Resource Publications
An Imprint of Wipf and Stock Publishers
199 W. 8th Ave., Suite 3
Eugene, OR 97401
www.wipfandstock.com

ISBN: 978-1-62564-784-9

Scripture quotations for selected poems are from THE HOLY BIBLE, NEW INTERNATIONAL VERSION® NIV® Copyright © 1973, 1978, 1984 by International Bible Society® Used by permission. All rights reserved worldwide

Quotations from Vincent van Gogh's letters appear by permission from Leo Jansen, Hans Luijten, Nienke Bakker (eds.) (2009), Vincent van Gogh - The Letters. Version: December 2010. Amsterdam & The Hague: Van Gogh Museum & Huygens ING. http://vangoghletters.org/vg/

Permission to reproduce letter excerpts and pictorial material was procured from the Van Gogh Museum Enterprises B.V. Van Gogh Museum Foundation, Amsterdam.

Manufactured in the U.S.A.

In memory of Johanna van Gogh-Bonger and Helene Kröller-Müller, who introduced Vincent van Gogh to the world through his letters and his art

Contents

Acknowledgments / ix
Preface / xiii
Bending Toward Heaven: Beginnings / xvi
Sunflower in the Garden / *xvii*

| I | *First Love* / 1 |

Roots / 3
Still Life with Bible / 4
Shepherd with His Flock Near a Little Church at Zweeloo / 5
Auction of the Crosses / 6
The Bearers of the Burden / 7
Prayer Before the Meal / 8
Child in Cradle with Kneeling Girl / 9

| II | *Painter of Peasants* / 11 |

The Potato Eaters / 13
Weaver Facing Left with Spinning Wheel / 14
Two Peasant Women Digging Potatoes / 15
Peasant Woman Sewing / 16
Peasant Woman with White Cap, Seated / 17
Old Man by the Fire / 18

| III | *People and Portraits* / 19 |

Sien with Cigar / 21
Sien with White Cap / 22
Sorrow / 23
Portrait of the Postman Joseph Roulin / 24
La Berceuse (Augustine Roulin) / 25
Marguerite Gachet at the Piano / 26
L'Arlésienne (Madame Ginoux) / 27
Self-Portrait with Dark Felt Hat / 28
Skull of a Skeleton with Burning Cigarette / 29

| IV | *Still Lifes and Growing Things* / 31 |

Still Life with Earthenware, Bottle and Clogs / 33
Vase with Poppies, Cornflowers, Peonies and Chrysanthemums / 34
Vase with Irises Against a Yellow Background / 35
Blossoming Almond Branches / 36
A Pair of Shoes / 37
Wild Roses / 38

V   *Holy Ground* / 39

The Angelus (after Millet) / 41
First Steps (after Millet) / 42
Morning: Peasant Couple Going to Work (after Millet) / 43
Noon: Rest from Work (after Millet) / 44
Evening: The Watch (after Millet) / 45
The Good Samaritan (after Delacroix) / 46
The Raising of Lazarus (after Rembrandt) / 47
Pietà (after Delacroix) / 48

VI   *Interlude in Arles* / 49

Vase with Fifteen Sunflowers / 51
Rocks with Oak Tree / 52
Willows at Sunset / 53
The Sower with the Setting Sun / 54
The Night Café / 55
The Yellow House / 56
Bedroom in Arles / 57

VII   *Bending Toward Heaven* / 59

Olive Trees with Yellow Sky and Sun / 61
Wheat Field with Cypresses / 62
The Irises / 63
A Corridor in the Asylum / 64
Wheat Field with Lark / 65
Starry Night / 66
The Church at Auvers / 67

VIII   *The Harvest* / 69

Heath with a Wheelbarrow / 71
The Harvest / 72
Red Vineyard at Arles / 73
The Large Plane Trees (Road Menders at Saint-Rémy) / 74
Landscape at Saint-Rémy / 75
Wheat Field with Crows / 76
On the Threshold of Eternity / 77
Sheaves of Wheat / 78

Credits:
Credits for art and letter quotations related to poems / 80
Additional references / 87

Acknowledgments

I gratefully acknowledge the following publications where poems from this book first appeared.

Common Threads: "Skull of a Skeleton with Burning Cigarette" and "Weaver Facing Left with Spinning Wheel"

The End of Summer: Y-City Writers Anthology. Zanesville, Ohio: "The Harvest"

First Things: "Child in Cradle with Kneeling Girl"

The Lost Country: "Still Life with Earthenware, Bottle and Clogs"

The Lyric: "Portrait of the Postman Joseph Roulin"

Modern Age: "First Steps," "Starry Night," and "The Good Samaritan"

String Poet: "Sheaves of Wheat"

Workshopping Our Words: Ohio Poetry Association Chapbook, and *Christian Research Journal*: "The Angelus"

I also wish to thank the following people associated with the Van Gogh Museum, Amsterdam. Fieke Pabst is editor of *Vincent van Gogh's poetry albums* and was Documentalist at the Van Gogh Museum Library when I made my first visit to the Netherlands in 2010. She patiently answered my many questions and introduced me to a treasure-trove of resources, especially the literary sources that inspired Van Gogh. Hans Luijten, with Leo Jansen and Nienke Bakker, edited the wonderfully annotated print and online editions of Van Gogh's letters; I discovered them after reading the three volume set of letters published in 1959 by the New

York Graphic Society. He gave me helpful advice on my return trip in 2014 related to referencing source material. Anita Homan, Van Gogh Museum Library Documentalist, helped me navigate through much needed reference material. Albertine Lykles-Livius in the Rights and Reproductions department assisted me with permissions. Special thanks to my husband and fellow poet, Scott Craig Mooney, and to the Ohio Poetry Association, the Pentapoets, Wordshoppers, and Write-On Writers of Coshocton, Ohio, and the poets on the *Able Muse/Eratosphere* online poetry workshop, for encouragement and critiques of various poems. Special thanks also to Jonathan Carlisle, Paulette Cadmus, Tom Daley, Terry Hermsen and Maj Ragain.

No, the heart that has truly loved never forgets,
But as truly loves on to the close,
As the sunflower turns on her god, when he sets,
The same look which she turn'd when he rose.

from "Believe Me, If All Those
Endearing Young Charms" —
The Poetical Works of Thomas Moore
by poet Thomas Moore (1779-1852)

Preface

Vincent van Gogh was a lover of poetry, though there is no indication in his voluminous correspondence that he wrote it himself. His letters to friends and relatives are laced with excerpts from the formal verse he had memorized. He also compiled poetry albums for his brother, Theo, and for the Dutch artist Matthijs Maris, and filled six pages of a visitors' book with fragments of poetry and prose.[1] Van Gogh's tastes ranged from poems of human love and human loss by Irish poet Thomas Moore to Dutch and evangelical hymns, Psalms, and the poetry of Henry Wadsworth Longfellow, John Keats, Christina Rossetti, Walt Whitman, and Jules Breton, a well-known and greatly admired French Realist painter of peasant themes.

While some historians and biographers imply that Van Gogh rejected a Judeo-Christian view of reality for other belief systems, including, though not limited to naturalism, pantheism and panentheism, his letters and his art do not support a total worldview shift, as a number of other authors have noted.[2]

To Van Gogh, nature was not the whole of reality; nor was nature God. Nature was poetry and unadulterated metaphor. The "convulsive, passionate clinging to the earth" of aged tree roots spoke to Van Gogh of the

---

1. See Fieke Pabst. Editor. *Vincent van Gogh's poetry albums Issue 1 of Cahier, Zwolle :Waanders/* Amsterdam: Rijksmuseum Vincent van Gogh, 1988.
2. See, for example, the following: Erickson, Kathleen Powers. *At Eternity's Gate: The Spiritual Vision of Vincent van Gogh.* Grand Rapids: Eerdmans, 1998; Davidson, Charles. *Bone Dead, and Rising: Vincent van Gogh and the Self Before God.* Eugene, OR: Cascade Books/Wipf & Stock, 2011; Vaux, Kenneth L. (Editor). *The Ministry of Vincent Van Gogh in Religion and Art.* Eugene, OR: Wipf & Stock, 2012; Havlicek, William J. *Van Gogh's Untold Journey. Revelations of Faith, Family, and Artistic Inspiration.* Amsterdam: Creative Storytellers. 2010; Wessels, Anton. *Van Gogh and the Art of Living: The Gospel According to Vincent van Gogh* (Henry Jansen, Translator). Eugene, OR: Wipf & Stock, 2013.

"battle for life." His landscapes, like his portraits, were meant to "touch people," often expressing "serious sorrow." In a row of pollard willows Van Gogh saw "expressions and soul." "We are surrounded by poetry on all sides," he wrote to his brother, reflecting on the "fantastically beautiful" and "curious skies" of winter. "With a thousand voices nature spoke to him...and his soul responded," wrote his sister Elisabeth. Van Gogh's paintings were an "echo" of nature's voice, his own artistic and poetic renderings of a created world spoken into existence by a Creator, speaking *to* him and *through* him.[3]

In his early years and then again in the months before his death, Van Gogh was drawn to the Bible. Initially his focus was on its words of hope and salvation, especially during the time when he served as a pastor-in-training and Protestant evangelist to the coalminers in the Borinage region of Belgium. Later he turned his attention to themes of daily rituals, manual labor, and to sowing and reaping as he moved from being a preacher to peasants to a painter of peasants. A final transition was to that of patient; he spent months in an asylum for the mentally ill. Yet it was in his state of forced confinement that Van Gogh did some of his best work, and where he turned his thoughts, as well as his art, once again to matters of the soul and spirit. His early "longings for the Lord" before he was rejected by the Church hierarchy (who thought him sadly lacking in expository skills) became, in his later years, identifications with Christ's sufferings. Initially viewed as a "light unto my path" and a "lamp unto my feet," the Bible as story became a "consolation" and object for

---

3. Selected words in quotes in the preface are from *The Complete Letters of Vincent van Gogh* (1959 second edition). Volumes I-III. Greenwich, CT: New York Graphic Society. Introduction by V.W. van Gogh. Preface and memoir by Johanna van Gogh-Bonger and from *Vincent van Gogh—The Letters*; Leo Jansen, Hans Luijten, Nienke Bakker (eds.) (2009), *Vincent van Gogh—The Letters*. Version: December 2010. Amsterdam & The Hague: Van Gogh Museum & Huygens ING. See Appendix for detailed references to letter quotations related to each poem. All are from the Van Gogh Museum & Huygens ING translation.

contemplation as he reproduced on canvas Delacroix's lithograph, *Pietà*, and Rembrandt's etching, *The Raising of Lazarus*. In both impastoed reproductions, the central figures resemble the artist himself.

Other than a single copying of a Rembrandt painting, and unlike some of his contemporaries like Bernard and Gauguin, Van Gogh did not believe in painting angels.[4] For Van Gogh, any winged spirits took the form of birds ascending in rainstorms or a celestial, glorious and radiant starry night. Yet Biblical themes abound. They took shape in concrete earthy forms rather than the numinous—a baby in a cradle that reminded Van Gogh of the "eternal poetry of the Christmas night with the infant in the stable," a shepherd guiding sheep past a country church, peasants praying in a field while Angelus bells toll in the distance, an old man with his head in his hands at the threshold of eternity, a sower casting seed on rocky soil, sheaves of wheat awaiting the final harvest, and sunflowers searching for the sun—bending toward heaven.

---

4. Cliff Edwards, in *Van Gogh's Ghost Paintings, Art and Spirit in Gethsemane*. Eugene, OR: Cascade Books/Wipf & Stock, 2015, presents a portrait of Van Gogh as "complex artist—religious seeker" and discusses Van Gogh's "ghost paintings" that did include an angel but were paintings he subsequently destroyed.

Bending Toward Heaven: Beginnings

The experiment of accepting the services of a young Dutchman, Mr. Vincent van Gogh, who felt himself called to be an evangelist in the Borinage, has not produced the anticipated results. If a talent for speaking, indispensable to anyone placed at the head of a congregation, had been added to the admirable qualities he displayed in aiding the sick and wounded, to his devotion to the spirit of self-sacrifice, of which he gave many proofs by consecrating his night's rest to them, and by stripping himself of most of his clothes and linen in their behalf, Mr. Van Gogh would certainly have been an accomplished evangelist. Undoubtedly it would be unreasonable to demand extraordinary talents. But it is evident that the absence of certain qualities may render the exercise of an evangelist's principal function wholly impossible. Unfortunately this is the case with Mr. Van Gogh. Therefore, the probationary period—some months—having expired, it has been necessary to abandon the idea of retaining him any longer.

From the 1879–80 report of the Synodal Board of Evangelization, Union of Protestant Churches in Belgium. Vincent van Gogh had been serving as a missionary to coal-miners and their families in the Borinage region of Belgium. Quoted in Van Gogh: *A Self-Portrait; Letters Revealing His Life as a Painter,* selected by W.H. Auden.

...despite the onset of winter, he continued to visit the miners and to give away whatever wretched clothing he had left and to pass on any food he could afford from the pittance his parents were occasionally able to send him...the Decrucqs (the couple Van Gogh rented a room from) pitied him but felt powerless to stop him...they could hear Vincent weeping to himself at night...(this event occurred following his official dismissal by the Synod). In *Van Gogh: His Life and His Art,* by David Sweetman.

Sunflower in the Garden
after Vincent van Gogh's
Allotment with Sunflower, 1887

They said that you were once a water nymph
Experiencing unrequited love
For the Greek god whose chariot raced above
The clouds and circled like a labyrinth,
Dispelling storms. Apollo had long since
Your affections spurned, and yet your thoughts of
Him stayed true. Like a lonely mourning dove
Your plaintive cries, your sobs sought to convince,
To turn affections round once more. Your head
Turned slowly back and forth across the sky
Searching for the sun, your heart misgiven.
Now you must realize past dreams are dead,
And though your first love said a cruel goodbye,
Lift your petals high and bend toward heaven.

I   First Love

Would you also ask for me that a way be found for me to devote my life, more so than is now the case, to the service of Him and the gospel? I continue to insist and I believe that I'll be heard, I say this in all humility and bowing myself down, as it were. Letter from Vincent to his brother Theo, 1877, Dordrecht, South Holland, The Netherlands

---

I cannot tell you how much I sometimes yearn for the Bible. I do read something out of it every day, but I'd so much like to know it by heart and to see life in the light of that word of which it is said: Thy word is a lamp unto my feet, and a light unto my path. I believe and trust that my life will still be changed, and that that longing for Him will be satisfied. Letter from Vincent to Theo, 1877, Dordrecht, South Holland, The Netherlands

---

I, for one, am a man of passions…For example, to name one passion among others, I have a more or less irresistible passion for books, and I have a need continually to educate myself, to study, if you like, precisely as I need to eat my bread. You'll be able to understand that yourself. When I was in different surroundings, in surroundings of paintings and works of art, you well know that I then took a violent passion for those surroundings that went as far as enthusiasm. And I don't repent it, and now, far from the country again, I often feel homesick for the country of paintings. Letter from Vincent to Theo, 1880, Cuesmes, Belgium

Roots

Half torn up by the storm, you aged tree
Still standing by the river on its bank,
You lean, and yet you cling so passionately
To the good earth, symbolic, like an ankh,
A weather-beaten talisman. Your roots,
Testy and knotted like an old man's cane,
Have served you well. Your branches involute,
Twist round each other, crying out in pain.
Arthritic limbs, of autumn's leaves stripped bare
Will shiver by the river when the snow
Comes. Then the cycle starts again. Take care.
Brave ice, and thaw; brave April winds that blow.
Though nature's enemies demand their toll,
They will not win the battle for your soul.

> *I wanted to express something of life's struggle,... in those gnarled black roots with their knots.*
> Letter from Vincent to Theo, 1882

Still Life with Bible

His father's Bible rests next to a book
And pewter candlestick in mellow shades
Of brown and white against a black backdrop.
And though it may be night, soft light cascades
Down open pages where a prophet's pen
Wrote of a tender plant who bore our grief,
Carried our sorrows, offered his soul for sin
That those estranged from God might find relief.
Émile Zola's *La Joie de Vivre* reveals
More modern tales of life and death it seems,
About an orphan girl who suffered and healed.
In both books joy and suffering, twin themes,
Are captured in this still life from traditions
Old and new, yet not in opposition.

> *For my part, I'm always glad that I've read the Bible better than many people nowadays, just because it gives me a certain peace that there have been such lofty ideas in the past. But precisely because I think the old is good, I find the new all the more so.*
> Letter from Vincent to his sister Willemien van Gogh, 1887

Shepherd with His Flock Near a Little Church at Zweeloo

Beside the country church the shepherd walks
On past a hedge that grows close to the ground.
There are no men or women standing around
This church today engaged in Sunday talk
About the sermon, then the price of stalks
Of wheat they'll sell at market Monday, bound
In sun-dried sheaves. Today there's not a sound
Except the quiet bleat of sheep who balk
At times and wander from the narrow way,
Seek grass that appears much greener than the grass
That's growing here next to the yellow fields
Of corn. But their good guide won't let them stray
Too far from home, knowing some paths they pass
Could lead to death. A rod and staff he wields.

I passed a little old church...just exactly the church at Gréville in Millet's little painting...but here, instead of the little peasant with the spade in that painting, a shepherd with a flock of sheep came along the hedge.
Letter from Vincent to Theo, 1883

Auction of the Crosses

They're pulling down the tower in the fields,
Auctioning lumber in the old churchyard.
It's been a long time since Sabbath bells peeled
To call the faithful; now they're trying hard
To outbid one another for slabs of slate
Or bits of iron lying on the ground,
And I am curious to know the fate
Of hand-hewn crosses scattered all around
That once stood proud and tall, that once graced graves,
But now are profit for the auctioneer;
Indeed the very thought that Jesus saves
Seems foreign to the crowd that's gathered here.
Everything's for sale and crows are flying
Around this scene of bidding and of buying.

> *The old tower in the fields is being demolished. There was a sale of woodwork and slates and old iron, including the cross.*
> Letter from Vincent to Theo, 1885

The Bearers of the Burden

Backs bent under full sacks the women came
Bearing the coal their husbands dug each day.
One held a lantern, one a twisted cane.
They passed a wooden shrine along the way
Nailed to a tree, their Lord upon His cross,
Gazing on them, eyes filled with empathy.
Thin, pale and weary, pictures of pathos,
And yet it's clear they sought no sympathy,
Their lives a pattern, circumscribed, confined,
With families to cherish, clothe and feed.
Each father labored, deep in dangerous mines;
Each mother prayed her children would not need
To live their lives as if under a curse
And die within the belly of the earth.

> *The workers there are usually people, emaciated and pale owing to fever, who look exhausted and haggard, weather-beaten and prematurely old, the women generally sallow and withered.*
> Letter from Vincent to Theo, 1879

Prayer Before the Meal

We see an aged peasant on an old
Oak bench, hands clasped; his worn hat rests next to
A table and a bowl of lentil stew.
It is the evening meal and in the cold,
Spare room, no one else is in this household
Save this man, whose tired head bends to review
The things he's thankful for now day is through.
On walls are shadows, tinged with sunset's gold,
Surrounding one who offers simple prayer
Rising like steam up from his wooden bowl,
Rising like incense, aromatic spice,
Pledge of allegiance to the One who cares
For golden censers filled with glowing coals,
For grateful hearts and humble sacrifice.

> *...I can fully share in it and even feel a need for it, at least in the sense that, just as much as an old man of that kind, I have a feeling of belief in something on high (quelque chose là-haut) even if I don't know exactly who or what will be there.*
> Letter from Vincent to Theo, 1882

Child in Cradle with Kneeling Girl

She has no gold, no myrrh, no frankincense,
Yet comes to him this night on bended knee
To rock his cradle, not a recompense,
But a gift to him. This is tranquility—
Small girl of five or six in a cotton dress,
A tiny infant sleeping with one hand
Grasping a blanket, warm against his chest,
Cheek resting on a pillow. Understand

There are no halos here, no angel wings
Like Botticelli painted, or Bernard,
And yet the hand that rocks the cradle brings
Us to a place where those of high regard
Bow down and worship, humbled at the sight
Of infinite inhabiting finite.

> *Yet if one has a need for something great, something infinite, something in which one can see God, one needn't look far. I thought I saw something—deeper, more infinite, more eternal than an ocean—in the expression in the eyes of a baby—when it wakes in the morning and crows (coos)—or laughs because it sees the sun shine into its cradle. If there is a 'ray from on high', it might be found there.*
> Letter from Vincent to Theo, 1882

II   Painter of Peasants

Paint us an angel, if you can, with a floating violet robe, and a face paled by the celestial light...but do not impose on us any aesthetic rules which shall banish from the region of Art those old women scraping carrots with their work-worn hands, those heavy clowns taking holiday in a dingy pot-house, those rounded backs and stupid weather-beaten faces that have bent over the spade and done the rough work of the world—those homes with their tin pans, their brown pitchers, their rough curs, and their clusters of onions. In this world there are so many of these common coarse people, who have no picturesque sentimental wretchedness! It is so needful we should remember their existence, else we may happen to leave them quite out of our religion and philosophy and frame lofty theories which only fit a world of extremes. Therefore, let Art always remind us of them; therefore let us always have men ready to give the loving pains of a life to the faithful representing of commonplace things— men who see beauty in these commonplace things, and delight in showing how kindly the light of heaven falls on them. George Eliot, in *Adam Bede*, 1859

After all, I desire nothing other than to live deep in the country and to paint peasant life. I feel that I can create a place for myself here, and so I'll quietly keep my hand to my plough and cut my furrow. Letter from Vincent to his brother Theo, April 1885, Nuenen, North Brabant, The Netherlands

The Potato Eaters

A family of five is gathered around
A wooden table where an oil lamp's glow
Casts shadows on a platter and a mound
Of new potatoes. This scenario
Is replayed countless times across the land,
Where days are filled with never-ending toil
That city-folk will never understand,
The symbiotic link twixt man and soil.
A painting of a cross hangs on one wall
Next to a clock that soon will toll the hour.
A grandmother pours coffee for them all
While forks reach out to spear and to devour,
Assuaging hunger. These of humble mien
Know that they've earned their food by honest means.

You see, I really have wanted to make it so that people get the idea that these folk, who are eating their potatoes by the light of their little lamp, have tilled the earth themselves with these hands they are putting in the dish, and so it speaks of MANUAL LABOUR and—that they have thus honestly earned their food.
Letter from Vincent to Theo, 1885

Weaver Facing Left with Spinning Wheel

He weaves a piece of sixty yards a week,
And while he weaves his faithful wife must spool,
Supplying his shuttles with her yarn. A cool
Breeze blows around this rustic cottage, seeks
To enter through the cracks. This couple ekes
A living from wool threads; the peasant's tool
Weaves cloth to sell for wood, the winter fuel
To warm his family. Gray pollards creak
Outside the window as the weaver throws
His shuttle, intersecting warp with weft
While patterns form within this gas-lit room.
The shuttle flies for hours to and fro,
Directed by strong fingers, long and deft,
Weaving red fabric on a brown oak loom.

> *As regards the work, I'm doing a fairly large painting of a weaver—the loom straight on from the front—the little figure a dark little silhouette against the white wall. And at the same time also the one I started in the winter, a loom on which a piece of red cloth is being woven...*
> Letter from Vincent to Theo, 1884

Two Peasant Women Digging Potatoes

Two peasant women dig in rocky soil,
Their bodies bent with spade and fork in hands
Calloused and worn from days of honest toil.
They seek to eke a living from the land,
Well-rounded women clothed in shades of brown
Like old potatoes covered with thick skin
Piled up in burlap baskets on the ground.

And when sun sets, these widows from Nuenen
Will gather up the fruits they've labored for,
Trudge slowly past high wheat fields with their sacks
Filled with their evening meal. At home, daughters
Are kneading dough for unleavened hard tack,
And putting kettles on to boil for greens
In this scene of the seen and the unseen.

> *I've also painted 3 more studies of the women among the potatoes, the first of which you've already seen.*
> Letter from Vincent to Theo, 1885

Peasant Woman Sewing

Inside the warm womb of her home she sat
Before a window on a wooden chair,
Hands resting and head bowed as if in prayer.
Her tired eyes now open to look at
The task at hand, some clothing on her lap,
A scarf perhaps or shirt needing repair;
Soon both will be the object of her care.
Long nimble fingers sew on buttons, tat
A lacy border for a christening gown.
Much like the proverbial woman, noble wife
Who never ate the bread of idleness,
This peasant woman's days are clothed and crowned
With dignity and strength; her quiet life
Reflects a humble conscientiousness.

*She watches over the affairs of her
household and does not eat the bread of
idleness.*
Proverbs 31:27

Peasant Woman with White Cap, Seated

How hard it is for me to pose, hands clasped
So tight before me, seated on this chair.
Others might think I didn't have a care;
They would be wrong, for I have many. Cast
Your eyes upon my hands; you'll see my past,
My present visible. My fingers wear
Thick calluses. Forgive me if I stare,
But I am thinking of the first and last
Important things today I need to do
Once this portrait is done—the bread to knead
And bake, more corn to plant in furrows deep
My husband's digging in the field. A few
More minutes I can spare, but then I need
To go. I've much to do before I sleep.

> *Still, I do believe that for portraits it's necessary to create a degree of comfort in a studio, otherwise the people who come to sit will dislike it.*
> Letter from Vincent to Theo, 1886

Old Man by the Fire

Head in his hands, his elbows on his knees,
The tired peasant sits on a pine chair
Pondering over life's uncertainties
Next to his hearth. A kettle hanging there
Swings like a bell that tolls the final hours
Of day or life itself. Nor do we know
What this old man with wooden shoes and dour
Expression on his face is feeling, though
There's no one else in sight, no wife, no son
to listen, comfort, or to help him shoulder
heavy burdens that he bears alone.
Fire turns to ash; the room grows colder.
This study of a man, weary and worn,
Reminds us that from dust we all were born.

> *... and finally an old, sick peasant sitting on a chair by the fireplace with his head in his hands and his elbows on his knees.*
> Letter from Vincent to Theo, 1881

III People and Portraits

I feel a certain power in me because, wherever I may go, I'll always have a goal—painting people as I see and know them. Letter from Vincent to his brother Theo, January, 1886, Antwerp, Belgium

---

And then—there's more and more demand for portraits—and there aren't so very many who can do that, and I want to try to learn to render a head with character. I've become particularly keen on this recently because my grasp of colour is becoming sounder. Letter from Vincent to Theo, November 17, 1884, Nuenen, North Brabant, The Netherlands

---

What I'm most passionate about, much much more than all the rest in my profession—is the portrait, the modern portrait. I seek it by way of colour, and am certainly not alone in seeking it in this way. I WOULD LIKE, you see I'm far from saying that I can do all this, but anyway I'm aiming at it, I would like to do portraits which would look like apparitions to people a century later. Letter from Vincent to his sister Willemien, June 5, 1890, Auvers-sur-Oise, France

Sien with Cigar

By an empty cradle and a full teapot,
A woman sits upon a hardwood floor,
Her eyes downcast, reflecting on her lot
In life, her reputation as a whore
Who wears, at times, the artist's choice of clothes,
Portraying her as patient seamstress, cook,
The wife he longs for, one he can compose,
Not one whose life has been an open book
For all to see. She sits with her cigar,
Inhales the pungent, earthy smells of home,
This small abode, and yet she's travelled far
And knows that soon she'll once more start to roam,
Return to walking lonely streets again
And think, with longing, of what might have been.

> *She has never seen, so to speak, what good was; how can she be good?*
> Letter from Vincent to Theo, 1883

Sien with White Cap

I wear this cap of domesticity,
And yet I'm really not the way I seem,
A woman of respectability;
That's not reality, only your dream.
Reality is that I've led a life
Of indiscretion, promiscuity,
And though you hope I'll change, become your wife,
Revise my ways, it's hopeless. Don't you see
That I'm not ready yet to settle down,
Forsake false loves for what I know is true?
So long I've been in darkness where I've found
No light can penetrate or filter through
The opaque lining of my hardened heart
That beats beneath this canvas of your art.

I have a sense of being at home when I'm with her, a sense that she brings my 'hearth and home' with her, a sense that we have grown together.
Letter from Vincent to Theo, 1882

Sorrow

Sorrow, he named you, and I contemplate
Just what it was that caused your nakedness
Of soul and attitude of mournfulness,
Loss so profound I would but hesitate
To say. Death of a mother, brother, mate,
Or sister? Or more likely fruitfulness
Has come to naught. Stillborn, is barrenness
What prompts your tears, bowed head, a grief so great?
In Ramah I am sure Rachel weeps still,
Lamenting loss that you can understand,
Mourning because her children are no more.
My prayer for you is that one day you will
Perceive the sorrow you have suffered can
Touch other hearts and meager hopes restore.

> *Whether in figures or in landscapes, I would like to express not something sentimentally melancholic but deep sorrow.*
> Letter from Vincent to Theo, 1882

Portrait of the Postman Joseph Roulin

One day, someone will say, clothes make the man,
And if they saw me posing here for you
Undoubtedly that statement might ring true.
But here is what you need to understand;
The rows of golden buttons, cap, bright bands
That decorate my coat of Prussian blue
Are public things and incidental to
The private person that I really am.
These clothes say I'm a postal employee,
Yet many roles serve to define my life:
Devoted father, friend to those in need,
Republican, a socialist and free,
A faithful husband to a loving wife.
It's not my clothes that make me, but my deeds.

> *Now I'm working with another model, a postman in a blue uniform with gold trimmings, a big, bearded face, very Socratic. A raging republican.... A more interesting man than many people.*
> Letter from Vincent to Theo, 1888

La Berceuse (Augustine Roulin)

He painted me to grace crude cabin walls
Of fishermen who sail the angry seas;
Each day they toil to feed their families.
They cast wide nets and often hear sharp squalls
Of violent winds and only see landfall
When dusk has fallen and those quiet lees
That shelter from harsh storms, no guarantee
They give of safety or of rest. The call
To cast again will come before sunrise.
Yet here I sit, gentle reminder of
Their wives and mothers whose long day is done.
I rock the cradle of my infant son.
They'll gaze on me and know the ones they love
Are softly singing soothing lullabies.

> ...*the idea came to me to paint such a picture that sailors, at once children and martyrs, seeing it in the cabin of a boat of Icelandic fishermen, would experience a feeling of being rocked, reminding them of their own lullabies.*
> Letter from Vincent to Theo, 1889

Marguerite Gachet at the Piano

Classically poised on your piano stool
With yellow hair upswept into a bun,
Slim hands now hover over keys. Bright sun
Lights up green painted walls. You know the rule
Of well-established forms you learned in school
Once played by Beethoven, Mozart, Haydn—
Sonatas, serenades steeped in tradition,
Expected in a lady's schedule.

But when long fingers strike we hear Baroque
From artists like Vivaldi, Handel, Bach—
Thick-textured notes much like your pearl-pink gown
That swirls around you in impastoed strokes,
As with rich-textured music you unlock
Bright colors from an instrument of brown.

> ...*Van Gogh was continually comparing the notes of the piano with Prussian blue and dark green and dark ochre, and so on, all the way to bright cadmium-yellow...*
> Anton Kerssemakers in the magazine *De Amsterdammeher*, April, 1912

L'Arlésienne (Madame Ginoux)

He posed her once with parasol and gloves,
Yet here she sits with books upon on a table
Enticing us to read if we are able
About life here below—of hatred, love,
Of slavery and the poor. Those who above
All else could separate a fact from fable,
Wrote from the heart. They penned most capable
Words rising like new bread or like a dove
To teach Madame Ginoux, Van Gogh and us
Of war and peace both on the soil and in
The soul. We read to find the common thread
That ties together separate worlds. No fuss,
No frills, just simple words: redemption, sin—
The first a promise when the second's dead.

> *I've re-read Beecher Stowe's Uncle Tom*
> *with EXTREME attention precisely because*
> *it's a woman's book, written, she says,*
> *while making soup for her children, and*
> *then also with extreme attention C.*
> *Dickens's Christmas Tales.*
> Letter to Willemien, 1889

Self-Portrait with Dark Felt Hat

Respectable in middle-class attire,
Felt hat, warm coat, blue tie, a well-clipped beard—
Rust-red, a sober hue. But where's the fire
In your gray eyes? I wonder if you feared
To show emotions running deep within
Your soul? Or were you saving them to paint
A cypress tree, a flower, or ragamuffin
Your heart responded to, or fields of grain
Burning beneath October's harvest sky?
No artist's smock, no signature straw hat,
No pipe, no missing ear, no slanted eye
In this portrait of self, your caveat:
Reflection of a longed-for ordered life
To circumscribe your world of stress and strife.

Here we have an unexpected view of Vincent van Gogh in respectable middle-class attire—very different from the artist's blue smock and straw hat.
Marc Edo Tralbaut in *Vincent van Gogh*

Skull of a Skeleton with Burning Cigarette

Dry bones you painted, anatomically
Correct, a skeleton devoid of flesh
And blood with burning cigarette. No fresh
Spring air, no vital physiology,
But just a study of anatomy,
Perhaps your own self-portrait, death enmeshed
In life. There is no garden here, no crèche,
No hopeful promise of eternity,
But only hills and valleys of dry bones,
Articulated framework waiting for
God's breath to enter in, awaken life,
Just like you did for others, making known
Strong peasant farmers, weavers, miners, more,
Embodied by your brush and palette knife.

> *He asked me, "Son of man, can these bones live?" I said, "O Sovereign LORD, you alone know."*
> Ezekiel 37:3

IV Still Lifes and Growing Things

He recognizes the ambrosia which nourishes his soul, in the bright orbs that shine in Heaven, in the volutes of the flower, in the clustering of low shrubberies, in the waving of the grain-fields, in the slanting of tall, Eastern trees, in the blue distance of mountains, in the grouping of clouds, in the twinkling of half-hidden brooks, in the gleaming of silver rivers, in the repose of sequestered lakes, in the star-mirroring depths of lonely wells. He perceives it in the songs of birds, in the sighing of the night-wind, in the repining voice of the forest, in the surf that complains to the shore, in the fresh breath of the woods, in the scent of the violet, in the voluptuous perfume of the hyacinth, in the suggestive odor that comes to him at eventide from far-distant, undiscovered islands, over dim oceans, illimitable and unexplored. Edgar Allan Poe in "The Poetic Principle," 1850

Poetry surrounds us everywhere... Letter from Vincent to his brother Theo, March 18, 1883, The Hague, South Holland, The Netherlands

---

I don't know if you'll understand that one can speak poetry just by arranging colours well, just as one can say comforting things in music. Letter to his sister Willhemien, November 1888, Arles, France

Still Life with Earthenware, Bottle and Clogs

No crystal glassware here, no fragile vase,
No linen, just a wooden table, bare
Of ostentation. Common earthenware
Instead, brick-red and rounded at its base
Stands by a crumpled cotton cloth. No lace,
No crocheted doily mats, but just one pair
Of wooden clogs carved from a tree. No chair
Is seen in this still life, yet there's a place
For wine to sit and gladden weary hearts
After the day is through and land is tilled.
Outside this frame a fire blazes bright;
A kettle boils. A wife waits to impart
Her simple gift of bread from flour milled
From grain her husband brings home every night.

> *...wine that gladdens human hearts, oil to make their faces shine, and bread that sustains their hearts.*
> Psalm 104:15

Vase with Poppies, Cornflowers, Peonies and Chrysanthemums

Who gave you leave to wander mornings through
Their gardens? There you must have gathered these
Bright orange poppies, blood red peonies,
White daisies, tiny cornflowers of blue,
Soft petals streaked with rain or dripping dew,
Arranged in a bouquet that would well please
A mother or a bride, or bring heartsease
To heartsick hearts. My needs today are few;
I want to rest awhile and gaze upon
Your flowers in this profligate still life.
Still others bloom around the vase's base.
I see wild pansies, gold chrysanthemums
Plucked from the womb of earth. They've been midwived
By you for me to view—a gift of grace.

>   *...simply flowers...*
>   from a letter from Vincent to the English
>   painter Horace Mann Livens, 1886

Vase with Irises Against a Yellow Background

They range from carmine to pure Prussian blue,
Spring irises, envased, inviolate,
Painted with care, the artist's billet-doux,
Each flower unique, a well-placed corollet
Of color, bright against a citron wall.

This still life on a canvas speaks of calm,
Of order rising from days held in thrall,
At times, to fits of madness like a storm.

Two personalities, but juxtaposed,
Yielded a life of complementary
Chromatic colors serving to transpose
Fugue-like existence to a major key
With gentle brushstrokes, not the palette knife,
Revealing wholeness in a broken life.

> *On the contrary, the other violet bouquet (ranging up to pure carmine and Prussian blue) standing out against a striking lemon yellow background with other yellow tones in the vase and the base on which it rests is an effect of terribly disparate complementaries that reinforce each other by their opposition.*
> Letter from Vincent to Theo, prior to his discharge from Saint-Rémy mental asylum, 1890

Blossoming Almond Branches

Green almond branches flower against sky,
Teal blue, a brilliant harbinger of spring.
This artist's gift acknowledges the cry
Of a newborn nephew whose appearance brings
Delight to those who waited for this son.
Perhaps he knew the story of the tree,
Of Phyllis, and remorseful Demophon
Whose tears birthed blossoms in mythology,
Or of the blooms that burst forth from the rod
Of Aaron, bearing almonds ripe and sweet
If Israel was faithful to her God.
Or possibly this graceful arboret
Grew once in Eden, nature's paradise,
And serves to represent the tree of life.

>*...I started right away to make a painting for him, to hang in their bedroom. Large branches of white almond blossom against a blue sky.*
>Letter from Vincent to his mother on the birth of his nephew to Theo and Theo's wife, Johanna, 1890

A Pair of Shoes

Heidegger wrote about these old worn shoes
In language hermeneutically hurled,
A reproduction of their essence, truths
About the peasant woman and her world.
"Oh no!" historian Schapiro said.
"These shoes are Van Gogh's shoes, it's plain to see;
They don't reflect the peasantry, instead
They mirror an artist's life, unlaced and free."

His fellow students, though, were less impressed,
And called his choice of subject "most bizarre".
It made more sense to paint the people dressed,
Or naked to hang up in the boudoir.

But I would beg to ask, "Why all this talk?
It's plain to see, these shoes were made to walk."

> ...what makes him so sure that they are a
> pair of shoes? What is a pair?
> Jacques Derrida in *Truth in Painting*

Wild Roses

With myriad voices nature spoke to you,
Reflecting, too, your personality,
Like the wild rose you painted—prickly,
Protecting leaves and stems from people who
Might want to move too close, because the view
Of delicate white flowers they could see
Would seem to indicate the fruit would be
Most sweet. I know you often seemed to rue
Dark times you lay tormented in your bed
By images unholy or unkind.
Outside your asylum window, light, though faint,
Did dawn; it warmed the earth that oft seemed dead
Yet teemed with growing things that would remind
Your soul to listen, and your brush to paint.

> *With a thousand voices nature spoke to him...and his soul listened...*
> Elisabeth Huberta du Quesne-van Gogh, sister of Vincent, 1910 in *Personal Memories*

V   Holy Ground

When I entered the room in Hôtel Drouot where they were exhibited, I felt something akin to: Put off thy shoes from off thy feet, for the place whereon thou standest is holy ground. Letter from Vincent to his brother Theo after viewing a sale of Millet's drawings, Paris, France, June 29, 1875

The figure of Christ has been painted—as I feel it—only by Delacroix and by Rembrandt... And then Millet has painted... Christ's doctrine. Letter from Vincent to the artist Emile Bernard, Arles, France, June 26, 1888

The Angelus (after Millet)

Holding his hat, the peasant farmer bows
His head. His wife beside him folds her hands
In prayer. A three-tined fork stands in the land,
Well-tilled, that yields up new potatoes;
Some fill a basket, others lie in rows
Upon the ground. We're meant to understand
The parish bell is pealing as a band
Of larks ascends into a sky that glows
With sunset's rays. The triple stroke repeats
Three times, nine peals to summon faithful folk
To cease from toil and contemplate the birth
Of Word made flesh. Day's work is now complete;
Now Angelus bells prompt them to invoke
The God who blesses virgin wombs and earth.

> *Yes, that painting by Millet 'The evening
> angelus' 'that's it'. That's rich, that's poetry.*
> Letter from Vincent to Theo, 1874

First Steps (after Millet)

How beautiful, Millet! I'll re-create
Your small white house, thatched roof, your apple tree
Arrayed in flowering blooms, your garden gate.
Your unpretentious domesticity
Has a young farmer dressed in faded blue
Kneeling beside his spade with outstretched arms,
Delighted with his child who is eager to
Explore the world beyond her mother's warm
Embrace, the garden of her father, though
For now all her attention is on him.
One tiny arm she flings, her face aglow,
Forsaking rhyme and reason for a whim.
Tottering steps, unguided, yet she knows
Safety lies with the one to whom she goes.

How beautiful the Millet is, A child's first steps!
Letter from Vincent to Theo, October, 1889

Morning: Peasant Couple Going to Work (After Millet)

Millet sketched them in muted somber tones,
A peasant couple at the break of day,
In charcoal—black and white with shades of gray.
They travel through a waking world, well known.
Thinking, perhaps, of his own life, lived alone,
Van Gogh revisited, sought to convey
In greens and blues and browns the interplay
Of man and wife, his criterion, touchstone.
This husband, three-pronged pitchfork in his hand,
Strides on with measured steps behind an ass
Bearing his pregnant spouse, who's saving strength won
To scatter seeds on fertile, furrowed land
Her husband harrowed through the rocks and grass.
Until this day is done, they'll toil as one.

> *You gave me very great pleasure by sending me those Millets. I'm working on them zealously. I was growing flabby by dint of never seeing anything artistic, and this revives me.*
> Letter from Vincent to Theo, 1889

Noon: Rest from Work (after Millet)

Man and wife rest when morning's work is done.
He's shed his shoes; sickles are by his side.
His straw hat shields him from the noon day sun
And winter wheat stands in the field beside
The wagon and the grazing cattle. Sheaves
In bundles tied with twine lie on the ground
Next to the farmer's wife. The shadows weave
A pattern of rich gold and sienna brown,
As they both drift off to sleep, perchance to dream,
These peasant farmers who work in the fields
From dawn to dusk each day. This is their theme:
Life lived each moment close to the soil yields
A harvest to enjoy, your daily bread
And then warm comforts of the marriage bed.

So working either on his drawings or the wood engravings, it's not copying pure and simple that one would be doing. It is rather translating into another language, the one of colours, the impressions of chiaroscuro and white and black.
Letter from Vincent to Theo, 1890

Evening: The Watch (After Millet)

From the bed-frame made of pine an oil lamp swings,
Casts multicolored shadows on the floor.
A cat curls by the fire and on a four-
Legged stool a father sits. The cold night brings
Him closer to the hearth as his wife sings
A lullaby to sooth the child she bore.
She sings, fervently prays God will restore
Their boy to health; they're not abandoning
Hope. She sits and sews and he, a weaver,
Weaves a willow basket, something to do
To pass the empty hours until the dawn
Creeps in to warm their world; and if fever
Should break, cold death will not intrude into
Their lives this day and sadness will be gone.

> *You know, one of the things I like best is the Evening after Millet. Copied like that it's no longer a copy. There's a tone in it and everything is so harmonious. It's really very successful.*
> Letter from Theo to Vincent on his brother's painting of the same work, 1890

The Good Samaritan (after Delacroix)

A wooden box stands open on the ground,
Empty of treasures, bandages perhaps
Soaked well in oil their owner used to wrap
Up bleeding wounds around this man he found
Beside the stream and road, where others bound
For worship walk on by, their periapts
And tassels keeping them from harm. With rapt
Expressions on their faces, not a sound
They make, nor do they heed the plight of one
Who's beaten, stripped of clothes and is the least
Of their concerns. Near death, he thought he saw
An angel, not a good Samaritan
Lifting him gently onto his own beast,
Attentive to the spirit of the law.

But a Samaritan...took pity on him.
Luke 10:33

The Raising of Lazarus (after Rembrandt)

The cave is gold with shades of green and white,
And there's a man who lies against the stones,
His eyes half open, gazing at the light,
A bright sun glowing, warming his cold bones
And bearded face. The grave clothes he still wears,
Though he no longer needs the handkerchief
That waves from the right hand of one who cares,
Amazement on a face once filled with grief.
Another woman, darker, smaller, frail,
Kneels by his feet and looks into his eyes.
These sisters seem alarmed at this man's pale,
Thin, wrinkled face, yet soon they'll see him rise
Like a coefficient of reflection,
And witness a brother's resurrection.

> *Jesus said to them, "Take off the grave clothes and let him go."*
> John 11:44

Pietà (after Delacroix)

Tradition says the mother holds the son
Descended from the cross. His nail-scarred hands
Are visible. The crucifixion's done;
The Christ is dead, we're meant to understand.
This was the image Michelangelo
First sculpted, Jesus lying on the knees
Of one who bears his lifeless form. Sorrow
And lamentation on her face are seen.

This Mary's hands, instead, are reaching out
Around her son, revealing inchoate
And yet true signs of faith. Renouncing doubt,
Embracing hope, she seeks to supplicate
The One with power and with predilection,
Who could answer with a resurrection.

*I am not indifferent, and in the very
suffering religious thoughts sometimes
console me a great deal.*
Letter from Vincent to Theo, when working
on the Pietà at in Saint-Rémy mental
asylum, 1889

VI Interlude in Arles

From the start, I wanted to arrange the house not just for myself but in such a way as to be able to put somebody up. Naturally, that ate up most of my money. With what was left, I bought 12 chairs, a mirror, and some small indispensable things. Which in short means that next week I'll be able to go and live there. For putting somebody up, there'll be the prettiest room upstairs, which I'll try to make as nice as possible, like a woman's boudoir, really artistic. Then there'll be my own bedroom, which I'd like to be exceedingly simple, but the furniture square and broad. The bed, the chairs, table, all in deal. Downstairs, the studio and another room, also a studio, but a kitchen at the same time. One of these days you'll see a painting of the little house itself, in full sunshine or else with the window lit and the starry sky. Then you'll be able to believe you own your country house here in Arles. Because I myself am enthusiastic about the idea of arranging it in such a way that you'll like it, and that it'll be a studio in a style absolutely meant to be that way. Let's say that in a year you come to spend a holiday here and in Marseille, it will be ready then — and the way I envisage it, the house will be just full of paintings from top to bottom. The room where you'll stay then, or which will be Gauguin's if Gauguin comes, will have a decoration of large yellow sunflowers on its white walls. Opening the window in the morning, you see the greenery in the gardens and the rising sun and the entrance of the town. But you'll see these big paintings of bouquets of 12, 14 sunflowers stuffed into this tiny little boudoir with a pretty bed and everything else elegant. It won't be commonplace. Letter from Vincent van Gogh to his brother Theo, September 9, 1888, Arles, France

Vase with Fifteen Sunflowers

Some have turned to rust; soon their seeds will fall
While others flower still, bright orange and gold.
Fifteen you painted in a vase, a call
It seemed to be, your signature in bold
Bright hues. You said Quost had his hollyhock,
Jeannin his peony, but sunflowers
Were yours as on the canvas you unlocked
Rich treasure, nature's bounty. For hours
You studied them and then tried to convey,
With simple brush strokes or the palette knife,
Their fragile lives of blossom and decay
Into an allegorical still life
For all who'd take the time to stop and see
Your study of both art and poetry.

> *You know that Jeannin has the peony,*
> *Quost has the hollyhock but I have the*
> *sunflower...*
> Letter from Vincent to Theo, 1889

Rocks with Oak Tree

Scattered on the steep hill under gray sky
Are rocks, for millennia warmed by heat,
Washed by spring rains and rounded by the feet
Of shepherds and sheep who daily walked the dry
And rugged land, searching for a supply
Of grass to graze upon. In summer, sweet
Briar and thistles wave, clutch the earth, compete
With wildflowers for the chance to grow. Nearby,
A turtle dove takes wing. A sturdy tree
Plants ancient feet into hardscrabble earth.
A solitary place, a scene about
Hardscrabble life, and yet there's poetry
Within this frame, seasonal rhythms—birth,
Growth, work, old age, and death. These stones cry out.

Poetry surrounds us everywhere...
Letter from Vincent to Theo, 1883

Willows at Sunset

All in a row next to the river's bank
They stand; old gray-green bark is gnarled and rough
Like callused work-worn hands. Today they drank
From waters flowing to the sea, enough
To quench their thirst. Unlike willows who weep,
Bent branches rise to meet the skies, appear
To supplicate while humble roots run deep
Beneath dark soil. The sun will disappear
From our view soon, though now its orange glow
Illuminates an autumn world of burnt
Sienna grass. This peaceful scene below
Reveals an ordered nature, a recurrent
Theme with pollard willows rising from the earth,
Blessing the fertile womb that gave them birth.

> ...and in all of nature, in trees for instance, I see expression and a soul, as it were. A row of pollard willows sometimes resembles a procession of orphan (almshouse) men.
> Letter from Vincent to Theo, 1882

The Sower with the Setting Sun

The farmer sows beneath the evening sun's
Bright golden globe, illuminating soil
Well tilled and broken by the laborer's toil.
This sower sows alone; the sower's sons
Have their own lives to live. When day is done
Perhaps they head for Arles where rivers coil
Around the city and the smokestacks spoil
The view of farms, their borders overrun
By concrete roads. Tonight the air is chill.
Beside a leafing tree he tosses seed
Upon the fertile ground. No rocks or thorns
Or birds this sower sees. Tonight he'll spill
His seeds of corn and wheat and cottonweed,
Wait patiently for seedlings to be born.

Now in your canvases there's a vigour which one certainly doesn't find in chromos (inexpensive colored woodcuts), in time that will become very fine as impasto, and certainly they'll be appreciated one day
Letter from Theo to Vincent after receiving "The Sower" and other paintings from Arles, 1889

The Night Café

To ruin oneself, go mad, commit a crime—
All possibilities for those around
The tables in this night café. The time
For rational discussion that abounds
In daylight hours is long past. We see
One couple contemplating an affair,
And two men plotting—perhaps a robbery;
Another soul is slumped over in his chair.

The bar's well stocked with spirits. Three gas lamps
Are burning brightly, casting a gold glow
On brick-red walls, a pool table, and damp
Night air ensures that this unstaged tableau
In Arles is very likely to replay
Just like this scene, in other night cafés.

> *In my painting of the night café I've tried to express the idea that the café is a place where you can ruin yourself, go mad, commit crimes.*
> Letter from Vincent to Theo, 1888

The Yellow House

This is the yellow house you wrote about
In letters to your brother and Gauguin.
This is the house you felt without a doubt
Would shelter artists who would look upon
The world as you did, fertile countryside
Ripe for the harvest by strong peasants who
Broke up their fallow ground and scattered wide
Small seeds of corn and wheat and rye that grew
In rows that soon would feed a family
Of five, some cattle, horses, deer and crows.
For you, nature itself was poetry
In hills around Arlesian farms that rose
To touch the clouds, Creation's mystery.
You alone saw what others failed to see.

> *It's painted yellow outside, whitewashed*
> *inside—in the full sunshine. I've rented it*
> *for 15 francs a month.*
> Letter from Vincent to Theo, 1888

Bedroom in Arles

Over a pine bed, washstand, and two chairs
Light filters through black shutters, partly closed.
Absence of stress reflective of repose
And rest or sleep the artist, with great care,
Hoped to convey to us. It has a spare,
Efficient look. Hanging on pegs are clothes—
A jacket and a hat. We might suppose
This is the bedroom of the artist where
He lays his weary head after a day
Out in his studio—orchards and fields.
And on the wall are portraits of his friends,
The painter Boch and soldier Milliet.
Inside a yellow house this small room yields
One simple message—to your soul attend.

> *In short, looking at the painting should
> rest the mind, or rather, the imagination.*
> Letter from Vincent to Theo, 1888

VII   *Bending Toward Heaven*

Perhaps the most wonderful passage in Uncle Tom's Cabin is the one where the poor slave, sitting by his fire for the last time and knowing that he must die, remembers the words

Let cares like a wild deluge come,
And storms of sorrow fall,
May I but safely reach my home,
My god, my Heaven, my All.

This is far from all theology—simply the fact that the poorest woodcutter, heath farmer or miner can have moments of emotion and mood that give him a sense of an eternal home that he is close to. Letter from Vincent to his brother Theo, November 27, 1882, The Hague, South Holland, The Netherlands

―――――

Have you read Whitman's American poems yet? Theo should have them, and I really urge you to read them, first because they're really beautiful, and also, English people are talking about them a lot at the moment. He sees in the future, and even in the present, a world of health, of generous, frank carnal love—of friendship—of work, with the great starry firmament, something, in short, that one could only call God and eternity, put back in place above this world. They make you smile at first, they're so candid, and then they make you think, for the same reason. The prayer of Christopher Columbus is very beautiful. Letter from Vincent to his sister Willemien, August 26, 1888, Arles, France

I have been to see your brother Vincent. I promised to tell you what I thought of him. I am sorry to tell you that I think he is lost. Not only is his mind affected, but also he is very weak and despondent. He recognized me but did not show any pleasure at seeing me and didn't ask about any member of my family nor anyone else that he knows. When I left him I told him that I would come back to see him; he replied that we would meet again in heaven, and from his manner I understand that he was saying a prayer. From what the porter told me, I think that they are taking the necessary steps to have him placed in a mental hospital. Please accept, Monsieur, the greetings of him who calls himself the friend of your beloved brother. Letter from the postman, Joseph Roulin, to Theo van Gogh, December 26, 1888, Arles, France

Olive Trees with Yellow Sky and Sun

Not a Christ of one's imagination,
Passive, praying, haloed, an abstraction;
Coarse reality was inspiration,
Empiricism yielding satisfaction.
The halo here is circling a sun
That shines in France on ancient olive trees
Like those in gardens near Jerusalem.
Their twisted branches cry in agony
In other Van Gogh prints of this same scene
Where skies are gray above red-ochre soil,
His metaphor, perhaps, for things unseen—
Betrayal in a kiss; while dripping oil,
Impastoed layers, vibrant energy
Evoke in us both mood and memory.

> *The thing is, I've been working this month in the olive groves, for they'd driven me mad with their Christs in the garden, in which nothing is observed.... What I've done is a rather harsh and coarse realism beside their abstractions, but it will nevertheless impart the rustic note, and will smell of the soil.*
> Letter from Vincent to Theo about the paintings of Gauguin and Bernard, 1889

Wheat Field with Cypresses

Gilded in gold the wheat field waves like sea
Tossed by an angry storm, while overhead
Clouds overwhelm blue summer sky. Widespread
Across the canvas, mountains rise. We see
Green cypress flames, in Ovid's epopee
A symbol made for mourning of the dead.
Here, earth and heaven undulate instead
With Van Gogh's trademark restless energy,
Revealing both the darkness and the light,
A world alive with color and with form,
Trees tapered like Egyptian obelisks,
Opposite, yet equivalent of bright
Sunflowers he once painted, variformed,
Reflecting nature's metamorphosis.

> *It requires a certain dose of inspiration, a ray from on high which doesn't belong to us, to do beautiful things. When I'd done those sunflowers I was seeking the contrary and yet the equivalent, and I said, it's the cypress.*
> Letter from Vincent to Theo, 1890

The Irises

Beautiful study, full of air and life,
He painted you the year before he died,
This man who roamed in gardens, sought to hide
Himself away. He left this world of strife,
Disorder, sadness; his dark life was rife
With pain, confusion, madness when the tides
Rose up, and yet this man, how hard he tried
To bring order from chaos. Now the knife
He'd used once to cut off his ear is gone,
Replaced by knives that spread oil paint in strokes,
Irises blue and white and waving bright
And bold and bearded like the one whose dawn
Arose on canvas. Nimble fingers coaxed,
Birthed vast arrays, virtual bouquets of light.

It's a fine study, full of air and life.
Letter from Theo to Vincent, 1889

A Corridor in the Asylum

Asylum doors swung open, then they closed
Behind you when the madness would begin
To claim your mind and heart. You entered in
And spent long months alone, misdiagnosed,
Misunderstood; yet those dark halls imposed
A quiet place for you to heal. Your kin,
Your friends thought often that the light within
Your life, your art, was dead, yet time transposed
This lie with winter's thaw and nature tucked
Sweet secrets in brown seeds, asleep until
Spring rains caused them to wake. Then you would pass
Long hours painting small wild flowers plucked
From loamy soil, aware that God could still
Restore new hope, nestled in blades of grass.

> *But anyway, I think I shan't urge you too much to read such dramatic books when I myself, returning from this reading, am always obliged to go and gaze at a blade of grass, a pine-tree branch, an ear of wheat, to calm myself.*
> Letter from Vincent to Willemien, Saint-Rémy Asylum, 1889

Wheat Field with Lark

Green stalks bend over, signaling the storm,
Mid-summer's wheat field blows in July winds;
The gale's so strong, it threatens to transform
This scene, yet there is also light within.
Above the wheat, below the clouds a bird
Begins to rise from ground and then takes care
To soar above the tempest undeterred,
Waxing melodious, singing in the air
A sweet sustaining song, as if to hold
The winds at bay, pierce the cloud-covered sky,
Seeking a heavenly home that will enfold
Her, keep her safe from harm. And so she'll fly
Away as fierce torrential rains descend.
Unbound and free the soaring lark ascends.

> *...it won't be long before the lark sings in the meadow again.*
> Letter from Vincent to Theo, 1883

Starry Night

On fire with zeal to save the lost, Van Gogh
Slept on a mat of straw and preached to poor
Coal miners, their kin, and others of low
Estate. Yet sensing life had something more
In store for him, he left that world behind
To study form, anatomy; his art
Could lead to God as well as words. A mind
Could bend toward heaven, following the heart
Into a flower bursting with the sun.
In later years he would hallucinate,
Yet still pursued his goal in an asylum,
And dreaming dreams transcendent he would paint
White clouds, a crescent moon, eleven stars
Ablaze with light, reflecting whose they are.

> *And it does me good to do what's difficult.*
> *That doesn't stop me having a tremendous*
> *need for, shall I say the word—for*
> *religion—so I go outside at night to paint*
> *the stars...*
> Letter from Vincent to Theo, 1888

The Church at Auvers

Gothic it stands, a church without a door
That once was open, symbol of the past,
Of days when he would read his Bible, fast,
Sleep on a mat, visit and clothe the poor
Miners he lived among. Often he wore
No shirt, no shoes. But charity, alas,
Was not enough, and so the die was cast.
The Synod said his excesses were more
Than what they'd bargained for. And though Van Gogh's
Probation as a pastor failed to please
The hierarchy who rejected him,
He gradually recovered from that blow,
Painted this church in Auvers-sur-Oise,
Brushing this canvas with his final hymn.

> *With that I have a larger painting of the village church—an effect in which the building appears purplish against a sky of a deep and simple blue of pure cobalt, the stained-glass windows look like ultramarine blue patches, the roof is violet and in part orange.*
> Letter from Vincent to Willemien, 1890

VIII The Harvest

As I watch'd the ploughman ploughing,
Or the sower sowing in the fields—or the harvester
    harvesting,
I saw there too, O life and death, your analogies:
(Life, life is the tillage, and Death is the harvest
    according.)
Walt Whitman in *Leaves of Grass*, 1900

———

It is an old faith and it is a good faith that our life is
a pilgrims progress—that we are strangers in the earth,
but that though this be so, yet we are not alone for our
Father is with us. We are pilgrims, our life is a long walk,
a journey from earth to heaven. Excerpt from Vincent
van Gogh's first sermon, at the Methodist Church in
Richmond, England, Sunday October 29, 1876

———

Sowing in the morning, sowing seeds of kindness,
Sowing in the noontide and the dewy eve;
Waiting for the harvest, and the time of reaping,
We shall come rejoicing, bringing in the sheaves.

Sowing in the sunshine, sowing in the shadows,
Fearing neither clouds nor winter's chilling breeze;
By and by the harvest, and the labor ended,
We shall come rejoicing, bringing in the sheaves.

Going forth with weeping, sowing for the Master,
Though the loss sustained our spirit often grieves;
When our weeping's over, He will bid us welcome,
We shall come rejoicing, bringing in the sheaves.

Hymn by Knowles Shaw, 1874
(Psalm 126:6, a Song of Ascents)

Heath with a Wheelbarrow

This Holland heath, uncultivated land
That stretches out far as the eye can see
In shades of olive, tossed beneath a sea
Of rain-soaked clouds and skies, this scene demands
We look more closely; deep in heather stands
An old wheelbarrow, waiting patiently
To be of use, but there's no guarantee.
The peasant's life of toil we understand
May yield, at times, potatoes, corn and beets,
Cabbage and kale, tomatoes on the vine,
Peat from the field to stoke the winter fires,
Grain for the harvest from the summer wheat,
Grapes in plump clusters, plucked to press for wine.
Abandoned cart could then be heart's desire.

The heath speaks to you, you listen to that still voice of nature, and nature sometimes becomes a little less hostile; ultimately you are her friend. Then your work is beautiful and calm too.
Letter from Vincent to Theo, 1883

The Harvest

A woman in her garden gathers greens.
A farmer in a wagon pitches hay
Next to a tall barn's loft; two ladders sway
Around a haystack, and blue hedgerows lean
In front of hills. It is late summer's scene
Of ordered industry. A trotting bay
Hitched to a heavy wagon makes its way
Across the fields; a distant road is seen
Connecting a French village to the farm,
A world where Van Gogh eats and sleeps above
Cafés, in a small, dark and shuttered room,
Then visits this world filled with grace and charm.
The artist comes to paint the things he loves,
Harvests of color bursting from earth's womb.

*Sometimes I can yearn for harvest time,
that is, the time when I'll be so permeated
by the study of nature that I myself will
create something in a painting...*
Letter from Vincent to Theo, 1882

Red Vineyard at Arles

From memory, after your evening stroll,
You painted this, a vineyard all in red.
Under a yellow sky a wagon rolls,
Drawn by a horse. The vineyard owner threads
His way around small gobelet vines
Dripping with heavy fruit; trained to climb round
Without support, their green leaves intertwine
Around strong wooden trunks of caramel brown.
A man walks down a muddy road, rain-drenched
And shining bright, as daylight fades. Like you,
He strolls on by, hoping perhaps to quench
His thirst for beauty. Dressed in shades of blue
Strong women bend under the setting sun
To harvest grapes, Grenache and Carignan.

We saw a red vineyard, completely red like red wine. In the distance it became yellow, and then a green sky with a sun, fields violet and sparkling yellow here and there after the rain in which the setting sun was reflected.
Letter from Vincent to Theo, 1888

The Large Plane Trees (Road Menders at Saint-Rémy)

He left the asylum and walked into the town;
The plane trees drew him there. Despite the cold
He pulled out his brushes, paused and looked around,
Then with impastoed strokes of autumn gold
He painted leaves to grace each graceful limb,
And blued their trunks with color by the road
Under repair by workmen. Picture him
Bearing the burden of a heavy load
Of mental anguish. Yet this peaceful scene
With solid blocks of concrete masonry
And women strolling by seems so serene,
In contrast to his restless energy—
A scene of workers diligently mending
Pavement under trees toward heaven bending.

In spite of the cold I'm continuing to work outside up to now, and I think that it's good for me and for the work. The last study I did is a view of the village—where people were at work—under enormous plane trees—repairing the pavements.
Letter from Vincent to Theo, 1889

Landscape at Saint-Rémy

Inside the wall that circumscribes his field
A farmer dressed in blue carries cut sheaves
Across the parched terrain. The stone wall weaves
Its way across the landscape like a shield
Between this peasant and the world revealed
Beyond, with streams and trees, heavy with leaves.
In the impastoed sky a cypress cleaves
A channel, like a flame. The artist wields
His knife, a scepter, calls forth roiling clouds
And mountain peaks that undulate like waves
Above the homes of relatives and friends
Who live and work beyond the wall. Their plowed
Fields yield rich harvests but this farmer braves
The elements alone, days without end.

In the foreground: A thistle and some dry grass. A peasant dragging a bundle of straw in the middle. It's another harsh study...
Letter from Vincent to Theo, 1889

Wheat Field with Crows

Interpreters all say his crows that fly
Are messengers of doom, and that Van Gogh
Was troubled so he painted troubled skies.
But should we take this bleak scenario
As gospel, or is there another tale
Told in his letters to his relatives
Of wheat fields, roads, and crows that just prevailed
On him to paint them "as they were"? He gives
Accounts, it's true, of instability,
Yet like the crows who hovered over wheat,
His landscapes show keen sensibility
To life. His final paintings were replete
With suns and moons and golden waves of grain,
Echoing boldly nature's true refrains.

> *...I see in my work an echo of what struck me, I see that nature has told me something, has spoken to me and that I've written it down in shorthand.*
> Letter from Vincent to Theo, 1882

On the Threshold of Eternity

There comes a tide in the affairs of man
When visions of the past come flooding in,
Of friends, of kin, good deeds that might have been.
These memories, like footprints in the sand,
Are evanescent, fleeting, but they can
Remind you of your need for discipline,
Reveal those things you need to reexamine,
Prompt you to finish what you once began.

Here, by the fire, head bent on clasped hands,
This aged peasant, lonely, tired, depressed,
Prays to his God, prepares his final plea.
The end of life is near, he understands;
This is the time to supplicate, confess,
Prepare for entering eternity.

Sad memory brings the light
Of other days around me.
from "Oft, In the Stilly Night" by Thomas Moore (poem quoted by Vincent in a letter to Theo for earlier lithograph), 1882

Sheaves of Wheat

You often painted fields of golden grain,
Canvas awash in morning's natural light,
With peasant men and women preordained
To reap the harvest, end of summer's rite,
A metaphor, the cycle of our lives,
Of small grains planted in soft fertile ground
Incubating, finally giving rise
To rows of wheat, young, waving and unbound,
Then gathered up in bundles at the end
Of day when fiery sunset fills the skies
And once-bright colors fade away and blend
To quieter shades that seem to sanctify
And bless earth's final scene. We should not grieve
The time of reaping, bringing in the sheaves.

> *What else can one do, thinking of all the things whose reason one doesn't understand, but gaze upon the wheatfields. Their story is ours...to be reaped when we are ripe...*
> Letter from Vincent to Willemien, 1889.
> Van Gogh completed Sheaves of Wheat a few weeks before his death in July, 1890

Credits for the Art and Quotations in the Text

Each poem reference includes the location where the painting, drawing or sketch was done and date completed, the medium/media used, the letter locations of any quotation in the text in the first parenthesis, the F and JH number book locations in the second parenthesis, the current location of the work of art and any additional identifying information.

Letter references used for the quotations that accompany poems and in the various book divisions are taken directly from *Vincent van Gogh—The Letters*; Leo Jansen, Hans Luijten, Nienke Bakker (eds.) (2009), December 2010. Amsterdam & The Hague: Van Gogh Museum & Huygens ING (http://vangoghletters.org/vg/). Included in the first parentheses is the Letter number from this online edition followed by the letter number from an earlier translation, *The Complete Letters of Vincent van Gogh*, published by Thames and Hudson in London in 1958, designated as CL in the reference. CL numbers also correspond to *The Complete Letters of Vincent van Gogh* published by the New York Graphic Society, Greenwich, Connecticut. The most recent translation from the Van Gogh Museum is believed to be the most accurate. I began my explorations into the life and art of Van Gogh through the earlier translations and believe they are well worth comparing.

Two books that contain visual reproductions of the majority of Van Gogh's paintings, drawing and sketches are *The Works of Vincent van Gogh: His Paintings and Drawings*, by Jacob Baart de la Faille and *The Complete Van Gogh: Paintings, Drawings, Sketches* by Jan Hulsker. The Van Gogh Museum and most other museums number Van Gogh's art using the letters F and JH to accurately identify each work of art.

The most comprehensive website to view the paintings, drawings and sketches of Van Gogh is The Vincent Van Gogh Gallery originally developed by David Brooks. See: http://www.vggallery.com. This website also includes F and JH numbers for most of Van Gogh's works and is an excellent resource that includes much biographical information.

Most museums also have websites and online access to the works of Van Gogh in their collections. In the course of writing poems for this book I was able to spend time in the Netherlands at the Van Gogh Museum and the Van Gogh Museum Library in Amsterdam, and the Kröller-Müller Museum in Otterlo, where many of Van Gogh's works reside. I also visited The Van Gogh Center in Nuenen, Netherlands and the Rijksmuseum (Museum of the Netherlands) in Amsterdam and have viewed Van Gogh's paintings in various museums in the United States. I have viewed color prints online and in various books obtained at museums. A listing of referenced and recommended books is included in this appendix and in the preface footnotes.

Sunflower in the Garden*: Paris, France, July 1887, oil on canvas (F 388v, JH 1307) Van Gogh Museum, Amsterdam, The Netherlands (Vincent van Gogh Foundation) *Also known as "Allotment with Sunflower" or "Garden with Sunflowers." In mythology, Clytie, a water nymph, experienced unrequited love for Apollo, god of the sun. In most versions of the myth, Clytie became a sunflower. Van Gogh's unrequited love for the church led to his becoming an artist.

I   First Love (Letter 106/CL 92; Letter 108/CL 88; Letter 155/CL 133)

Roots*: The Hague, The Netherlands, April 1882, pencil, chalk, ink, watercolor (Letter 222/CL 195) (F 933r, JH 142) Kröller-Müller Museum, Otterlo, The Netherlands *Also known as "Tree Roots in a Sandy Ground" or "Study of a Tree" and "Les Racines"
Still Life with Bible: Nuenen, The Netherlands, October 1885, oil on canvas (Letter 574/CL W1) (F 117, JH 946) Van Gogh Museum, Amsterdam, The Netherlands (Vincent van Gogh Foundation)
Shepherd with Flock Near a Little Church at Zweeloo: Drenthe, The Netherlands, November 1883, pen and pencil (Letter 402/CL 340) (F 877, JH 423) Private Collection

Auction of the Crosses*: Nuenen, The Netherlands, May 1885, watercolor (Letter 502/CL 408) (F 1230; JH 770) Van Gogh Museum, Amsterdam, The Netherlands (Vincent van Gogh Foundation) *Also known as "Sale of Building Scrap"

The Bearers of the Burden*: Brussels, Belgium, April 1881, pencil, pen and brush (Letter 151/CL 129) (F 832, JH no number) Kröller-Müller Museum, Otterlo, The Netherlands *Also known as "Miners' Women Carrying Sacks"

Prayer Before the Meal: The Hague, The Netherlands, December 12–18, 1882, pencil, chalk, ink (Letter 294/CL 253) (F 1002, JH 281) Private Collection

Child in Cradle with Kneeling Girl*: The Hague, The Netherlands, March 1883, pencil, black chalk, watercolor on paper (Letter 292/CL 242) (F 1024, JH 336) Van Gogh Museum, Amsterdam, The Netherlands (Vincent van Gogh Foundation) *Also known as "Girl Kneeling by a Cradle"

II   Painter of Peasants (Letter 490/CL 398)

The Potato Eaters: Nuenen, The Netherlands, April-May 1885, oil on canvas (Letter 497/CL 404) (F 82, JH 764) Van Gogh Museum, Amsterdam, The Netherlands (Vincent van Gogh Foundation)

Weaver Facing Left with Spinning Wheel: Nuenen, The Netherlands, March 1884, oil on canvas(Letter 445/CL 367 (F 29, JH 471) Museum of Fine Arts, Boston, Massachusetts, USA

Two Peasant Women Digging Potatoes: Nuenen, The Netherlands, August 1885, oil on canvas (Letter 529/CL 421) (F 97, JH 876) Kröller-Müller Museum, Otterlo, The Netherlands

Peasant Woman Sewing: Nuenen, The Netherlands, March-April 1885, oil on canvas (F 71, JH 719) Van Gogh Museum, Amsterdam, The Netherlands (Vincent van Gogh Foundation)

Peasant Woman with White Cap, Seated: Nuenen, March 1885, oil on canvas (Letter 556/CL 454) (F 144a, JH 704) Noordbrabants Museum, Den Bosch, The Netherlands

Old Man by the Fire*: Etten, The Netherlands, September 1881, pen and watercolor (Letter 172/CL 150) (F 863, JH 34) Amsterdam, The Netherlands (Collection of P. and N. de Boer Foundation) *Also known as "Worn Out"

III   People and Portraits (Letter 552/CL 444; Letter 470/CL 386; Letter 879, CL W22)

Sien with Cigar: The Hague, The Netherlands, April 1882, pencil, black chalk, pen, brush, sepia (Letter 379/CL 317) (F 898; JH 141) Kröller-Müller Museum, Otterlo, The Netherlands

Sien with White Cap: The Hague, The Netherlands, December 1882, pencil, black lithographic (Letter 244/CL 212) (F 931, JH 291) Van Gogh Museum, Amsterdam, The Netherlands (Vincent van Gogh Foundation)

Sorrow: The Hague, The Netherlands, November 1882, lithographic (Letter 249/CL 218) (F 1655-001, JH 259) Van Gogh Museum, Amsterdam, The Netherlands (Vincent van Gogh Foundation)

Portrait of the Postman Joseph Roulin: Arles, France, August 1888, oil on canvas (Letter 652/CL 516) (F 432; JH 1522) Museum of Fine Arts, Boston, Massachusetts, USA

La Berceuse (Augustine Roulin): Arles, France. February 1889, oil on canvas (Letter 743/CL 574) (F 508, JH 1671) Museum of Fine Arts, Boston, Massachusetts, USA

Marguerite Gachet at the Piano: Auvers-sur-Oise, France, June 1890, oil on canvas (Letter 683/CL 435c) (F 772, JH 2048) Offentliche Kunstsammlung-Kunstmuseum, Basel, Switzerland

L'Arlésienne (Madame Ginoux): Saint-Rémy-de-Provence, France, February 1890, oil on canvas (Letter 764/CL W11) (F 541, JH 1893) Kröller-Müller Museum, Otterlo, The Netherlands

Self-Portrait with Dark Felt Hat: Paris, France, December 1886, January 1887, oil on canvas (F 208a, JH 1089) Van Gogh Museum, Amsterdam, The Netherlands (Vincent van Gogh Foundation)

Skull of a Skeleton with a Burning Cigarette*: Antwerp, Belgium, January-February 1886, oil on canvas (F 212, JH 999) Van Gogh Museum, Amsterdam, The Netherlands (Vincent van Gogh Foundation) *Also known as "Head of a Skeleton with Burning Cigarette"

IV Still Lifes and Growing Things (Letter 330/CL 276; Letter 720/CL W9)

Still Life with Earthenware, Bottle and Clogs: Nuenen, The Netherlands, September 1885, oil on canvas (F 63, JH 920) Kröller-Müller Museum, Otterlo, The Netherlands

Vase with Poppies, Cornflowers, Peonies and Chrysanthemums: Paris, France, summer, 1886, oil on canvas (Letter 569/CL 459a) (F 278, JH 1103) Kröller-Müller Museum, Otterlo, The Netherlands

Vase with Irises against a Yellow Background: Saint-Rémy-de-Provence, France, May 1890, oil on canvas (Letter 870/CL 633) (F 678, JH 1977) Van Gogh Museum, Amsterdam, The Netherlands (Vincent van Gogh Foundation)

Blossoming Almond Branches*: Saint-Rémy-de-Provence, France, February 1890, oil on canvas (Letter 855/CL 627) (F 671, JH

1891) Van Gogh Museum, Amsterdam, The Netherlands (Vincent van Gogh Foundation) *Also known as "Blossoming Almond Tree"

A Pair of Shoes: Paris, France, September–November, 1886, oil on canvas (F 255, JH 1124) Van Gogh Museum, Amsterdam, The Netherlands (Vincent van Gogh Foundation)

Wild Roses: Saint-Rémy-de-Provence, France, May–June 1889, oil on canvas (F 597, JH 2011) Van Gogh Museum, Amsterdam, The Netherlands (Vincent van Gogh Foundation)

V   Holy Ground (Letter 036/CL 29; Letter 632/CL B8)

The Angelus (after Millet): Brussels, Belgium, October 1880, red chalk and pencil (Letter 017/CL 13) (F 834, JH Juv. 14) Kröller-Müller Museum, Otterlo, The Netherlands

First Steps (after Millet) Saint-Rémy-de-Provence, France, January 1890, oil on canvas (Letter 815/CL 611) (F 668, JH 1883) Metropolitan Museum of Art, New York, New York, USA

Morning: Peasant Couple Going to Work (after Millet): Saint-Rémy-de-Provence, France, January 1890, oil on canvas (Letter 816/CL 613) (F 684, JH 1880).Hermitage Museum, St. Petersburg, Russia

Noon: Rest from Work (after Millet): Saint-Rémy-de-Provence, France, January 1890, oil on canvas (Letter 839/CL 623) (F 686, JH 1881) Musée d'Orsay, Paris, France

Evening: The Watch (after Millet): Saint-Rémy-de-Provence, France, October–November 1889, oil on canvas (Letter 838/CL T24) (F 647, JH 1834) Van Gogh Museum, Amsterdam, The Netherlands (Vincent van Gogh Foundation)

The Good Samaritan (after Delacroix): Saint-Rémy-de-Provence, France, May 1890, oil on canvas (F 633, JH 1974) Kröller-Müller Museum, Otterlo, The Netherlands

The Raising of Lazarus (after Rembrandt): Saint-Rémy-de-Provence, France, May 1890, oil on paper (F 677, JH 1972) Van Gogh Museum, Amsterdam, The Netherlands (Vincent van Gogh Foundation)

Pietà (after Delacroix: Saint-Rémy-de-Provence, France, September 1889, oil on canvas (Letter 801/CL 605) (F 630, JH 1775) Van Gogh Museum, Amsterdam, The Netherlands (Vincent van Gogh Foundation)

VI   Interlude in Arles (Letter 677/CL 534)

Vase with Fifteen Sunflowers: Arles, France, August 1888, oil on canvas (Letter 741/CL 573) (F 454, JH 1562) National Gallery, London, England

Rocks with Oak Tree: Arles, France, July 1888, oil on canvas (Letter 330/CL 276) (F 466, JH 1489) The Museum of Fine Arts, Houston, Texas, USA

Willows at Sunset: Arles, France, Autumn 1888, oil on cardboard (Letter 292/CL 242) (F 572, JH 1597) Kröller-Müller Museum, Otterlo, The Netherlands

The Sower with the Setting Sun: Arles, France, June 1888, oil on canvas (Letter 774/CL T9) (F 422, JH 1470) Kröller-Müller Museum, Otterlo, The Netherlands

The Night Café: Arles, France, September 1888, oil on canvas (Letter 677/CL 534) (F 463, JH 1575) Yale University Art Gallery, New Haven, Connecticut, USA

The Yellow House: Arles, France. September 1888, oil on canvas (Letter 602/CL 480) (F 464, JH 1589) Van Gogh Museum, Amsterdam The Netherlands (Vincent van Gogh Foundation)

Bedroom in Arles*: Arles, France, October 1888, oil on canvas (Letter 705/CL 554) (F 482, JH 1608) Van Gogh Museum, Amsterdam The Netherlands (Vincent van Gogh Foundation) *Also known as "Vincent's Bedroom in Arles"

VII Bending Toward Heaven (Letter 288/CL 248; Letter 670, CLW8); Joseph Roulin. Letter to Theo van Gogh. Translated/edited by Robert Harrisonhttp://www.webexhibits.org/vangogh/letter/19/etc-Roulin-1-Theo.htm)

Olive Trees with Yellow Sky and Sun: Saint-Rémy-de-Provence, France, November 1889, oil on canvas (Letter 823/CL 615) (F 710, JH 1856) Minneapolis Institute of Art, Minneapolis, Minnesota, USA

Wheat Field with Cypresses: Saint-Rémy-de-Provence, France, June 1889, oil on canvas (Letter 850/CL 625) (F 717, JH 1756) Metropolitan Museum of Art, New York, New York, USA

The Irises: Saint-Rémy-de-Provence, France, May 1889, oil on canvas (Letter 799/CL T16) (F 608, JH 1691) J. Paul Getty Museum, Los Angeles, California, USA

A Corridor in the Asylum: Saint-Rémy-de-Provence, France, September 1889, watercolor, black chalk and gouache (Letter 785/CL W13) (F 1529, JH 1808) Metropolitan Museum of Art, New York, New York USA

Wheat Field with Lark*: Paris, France, June–July 1887, oil on canvas (Letter 308/CL 264) (F 310, JH 1274) Van Gogh Museum, Amsterdam, The Netherlands (Vincent van Gogh Foundation) *This painting has been renamed "Wheat Field with Partridge" based on closer analysis; Wheat Field with Lark is the title in all publications prior to 2011.

Starry Night: Saint-Rémy-de-Provence, France, June 1889, oil on canvas (Letter 691/CL 543) (F 612, JH 1731) The Museum of Modern Art, New York, New York, USA

The Church at Auvers: Auvers, France, June 1890, oil on canvas (Letter 879/CL W22) (F 789, JH 2006) Musée d'Orsay, Paris, France

VIII   The Harvest (Letter 096/CL 79)

Heath with a Wheelbarrow: Drenthe, The Netherlands, September 1883, watercolor and gouache (Letter 396/CL 339) (F 1100, JH 400) Cleveland Museum of Art, Cleveland, Ohio, USA

The Harvest: Arles, France, June 1888, oil on canvas (Letter 266/CL 233) (F 412, JH 1440) Van Gogh Museum, Amsterdam, The Netherlands (Vincent van Gogh Foundation)

Red Vineyard at Arles: Arles, France, November 1888, oil on canvas (Letter 717/CL 559) (F 495, JH 1626) Pushkin Museum, Moscow, Russia

The Large Plane Trees (Road Menders at Saint-Rémy) oil on fabric, Saint-Rémy-de-Provence, France, November, 1889 (Letter 824/CL 618) (F 657, JH 1860) Cleveland Museum of Art, Cleveland, Ohio, USA

Landscape at St Rémy*: Saint-Rémy-de-Provence, France, October, 1889, oil on canvas (Letter 810/CL 610) (F 641, JH 1795).Indianapolis Museum of Art, Indianapolis, Indiana, USA *Also known as "Enclosed Wheat Field with Peasant"

Wheat Field with Crows: Auvers-sur-Oise, France, July 1890, oil on canvas (Letter 260/CL 228) (F 779, JH 2117) Van Gogh Museum, Amsterdam (Vincent van Gogh Foundation)

On the Threshold of Eternity*: Saint-Rémy-de-Provence, France, April-May 1890, oil on canvas (Letter 294/CL 253) (F 702, JH 1967) Kröller-Müller Museum, Otterlo, The Netherlands. * Also known as "Old Man in Sorrow"

Sheaves of Wheat: Auvers-sur-Oise, France, July 1890, oil on canvas (Letter 785/CL W13) (F 771, JH 2125) Dallas Museum of Art (The Wendy and Emery Reves Collection) Dallas, Texas, USA

Primary References for Art and Quotations:

Auden, W.H. *Van Gogh: A Self-Portrait. Letters Revealing His Life as a Painter.* Selected by W.H. Auden. New York: Marlowe & Company, 1994

The Complete Letters of Vincent van Gogh (1959 second edition). Volumes I-III. Greenwich, CT: New York Graphic Society. Introduction by V.W. van Gogh. Preface and memoir by Johanna van Gogh-Bonger

de la Faille, Jacob Baart. *The Works of Vincent van Gogh: His Paintings and Drawings.* Reynal & Company in association with William Morrow & Company. First Revised Augmented Edition edition (1970).

Eliot, George. *Adam Bede.* 1859. See Project Gutenberg online. http://www.gutenberg.org/files/507/507-h/507-h.htm

Hulsker, Jan. *The Complete Van Gogh: Paintings, Drawings, Sketches.* New York: Harry N. Abrams, Inc., 1980.

Moore, Thomas. *The Poetical Works of Thomas Moore.* New York: Hurst and Company (c. 1880's–1890's)

Poe, Edgar Allan. "The Poetic Principle" in *Essays and Reviews.* New York: The Library of America. Literary Classics of the United States, Inc.,1984.

Sweetman, David. *Van Gogh: His Life and His Art.* New York: New York: Crown Publishers, Inc., 1990.

Tralbaut, Marco Edo. *Vincent van Gogh.* New York: Studio Book. The Viking Press, 1969.

Vincent van Gogh—The Letters; Leo Jansen, Hans Luijten, Nienke Bakker (eds.) (2009), *Vincent van Gogh—The Letters.* Version: December 2010. Amsterdam & The Hague: Van Gogh Museum & Huygens ING. http://vangoghletters.org.

Whitman, Walt. *Leaves of Grass.* Philadelphia: David McKay. 1900.

www.ingramcontent.com/pod-product-compliance
Lightning Source LLC
Chambersburg PA
CBHW070303100426
42743CB00011B/2323